A Scent of Pines

Jill Nevile

A Scent of Pines

Acknowledgements

Many of the poems in this collection – sometimes in a different form – have previously been published in the following:
Five Bells, *The Mozzie*, *Yellow Moon*, *The Dawn*, *Peninsula News*, *Multi Arts Confederation News Sheet*, *The Lady* (UK).

Poems have also appeared in the following anthologies published by Central Coast Poets Inc:
Suburbs of the Mind (2004), *Mood Cumulus* (2006), *Leaving the Bow* (2008).

Other poems have featured in the following UK anthologies:
Poetry Now Anthology, South East Vol. 1 (1990),
The Best of Poetry Now (1991), *Poetry Now*, Central (1992),
Poetry Now Regional Anthologies, London (1993),
Pleasure and Pain (Arrival Press, 1994),
Voices from the Heart of England (Anchor Books, 1995),
Love Lines (Poetry Now, 1995).

'To Her Bold Lover' was highly commended in the Internal Competition 2005 of Central Coast Poets Inc., adjudicated by external judges

A Scent of Pines
ISBN 978 1 74027 631 3
Copyright © Jill Nevile 2010
Cover photo: Temple of Hera, Samos, Greece, by Jill Nevile

First published 2010
Reprinted 2015

GINNINDERRA PRESS
PO Box 3461 Port Adelaide SA 5015
www.ginninderrapress.com.au

Contents

Special Places	9
Magnetic Greece	11
The Scent of Pines	12
The Pines of Spetses	13
Picnic At Nourlangie Rock	14
Roebuck Moon	15
The Call of the Kookaburra	16
Summer At Ettalong	17
The Faraway Grave	18
Cargo	19
A Personal Affair	21
Achilles Heel	23
Dancing With Fire	24
Just a Taste	26
A Disturbing Drive	27
Betrayed	28
The Meeting	29
Dream Lover	30
Invitation To a Dance	31
Honey For Tea	32
The Ruby Affair	33
To Her Bold Lover	34
Epitaph	35
The Empty Shell	36
Go In Peace	37
Intruder	38
Metamorphosis	39
The Kindness of Memory	40
To Maddie	41

Out and About — 43

- The Bondi Minotaurs — 45
- Little Wattlebird — 46
- Snack Lunch — 47
- Flamingo Lake — 48
- The Call of the Sea — 49
- Dressed To Thrill — 50
- The Magpie Choir — 51
- Across the River — 53
- Ode To Bright Eyes — 54

Lighter Notes — 55

- The Reluctant Valentine — 57
- Georgy's Duties — 58
- Limericks — 59
- Highway Cheer — 60
- Ode To Usury — 61
- Mammoth Creation — 62
- Life Is Too Short To Clean the Ridges — 63
- Creative Juice — 64

For all my friends, both old and new –

you have enriched my life

Special Places

Magnetic Greece

It drew me south from a land of frost,
With promises of warmth and well-being,
      To sit in tavernas, toes in the sand,
      Eat succulent, plump tomatoes,
      Watch the patchwork of harbour boats,
      With the evening breeze on my skin,
           And I succumbed.

It draws me north from a land of sun,
With promises of places unexplored,
      The tap of donkey hooves on cobbled streets,
      Landscapes of baked beauty,
      Silver fish with lemon from the groves
      That perfumed my morning walk,
           And I surrender.

The Scent of Pines

It started last year,
A familiar yearning
For walks through the olive groves,
Lingering over lunches
        with wine and watermelon,
The churring of cicadas,
Fresh fish in shady tavernas
        with the music of bouzouki

And the scent of pines.

For the bells of the goats,
Dolphins that follow the ferries,
A warm breeze on my cheeks,
The simple life where bread, cheese
        and olives are a feast,
For Greece – the land that
        draws me back
To its sparkling shores.

This year I will return.

The Pines of Spetses

All I had longed for –

Walks beside the olive groves,
Crescendos of crickets,
Bicycling down shady lanes
Lined with wild azaleas,
A cool breeze on my cheeks,
Birdsong in my ears,
Tastes of wine and watermelon,
And always, everywhere,
Permeating perception,

The scent of pines.

Picnic At Nourlangie Rock

After the picnic
We climbed the towering rock
To see the cave paintings.
Five of us started out.

A fleet-footed pair
Strode swiftly upward,
Speaking softly
In the hush of heat.

No bird called.
No breeze disturbed
Enveloping stillness.

I looked around.
The two who were behind
No longer followed.
The pair in front
Had disappeared.

                Alone
          In an eerie silence
On the side of an ancient rock
Amid a spreading wilderness
In a vast and distant continent
On the far side of the world.

Roebuck Moon

Night prepared the stage,
A backdrop of stars in a black sky,
An audience of hushed spectators.

At the appointed time
I peeped over the horizon,
The watchers were waiting.
In a costume of ochre light
I started my show.

Slowly I rose, revealing my fullness,
Until my blushing orb overlooked the bay.
The tide, my stage manager,
Had left the beach uncovered.

It was time for my grand finale.

I spread my light on the mud flats.
Glowing ripples beneath me
Made steps in the sand.
I held my audience with illusion,
They knew the bay was level,
But their eyes saw a sloping wonder –
A staircase to the moon.

The Call of the Kookaburra

I listened to tales of a far southern country
Washed by the surf and dried by the sun,
Tropical islands, red desert and outback,
In childhood Australia beckoned to me,
        I heard the call of the kookaburra.

Stories I read of pioneer people,
Explorers and miners, farmers and wives,
Vast cattle stations with thousands of acres,
Tough, rugged stockmen riding the trails,
        I heard the crack of the whipbird.

Years later I went to the far southern ocean
To visit the land of childhood romance.
I warmed to its people, candid and cordial,
Admired its remarkable animal life,
        I heard the cry of the currawong.

On every return to the faraway country
I capture the magic I felt as a child,
Riding the outback on strong mountain pony,
Cresting the waves on the soft, silky sands,
        I hear the song of the magpie.

Always drawn back to the shores of Australia,
To sample its splendour and savour its space,
Enjoy the sensation of limitless landscape,
Gaze at night skies encrusted with stars,
        I hear the call of the kookaburra.

Summer At Ettalong

In a haze of heat
The beach stretches and curves
Around a satin sea.
Sunbakers laze on the sand,
Babies slumber; dogs snooze
Away the afternoon.
Swimmers float in the cooling water,
Youngsters sit on rocks dangling feet
And watch the ferry glide through glass.
Fishermen stand knee-deep
In the ocean, but the fish
Rest in the depths.
Picnickers, sheltering in the shade,
Speak softly in the hush
Of summer at the bay.

The Faraway Grave

Isolated, far from home,
I lie beside the bay,
The mighty ocean at my feet
Prevented all escape.

Condemned to leave my native land,
Australia was my jail,
But misdemeanours such as mine
Brought harsher punishment.

Banished to Norfolk Island,
That hell in paradise,
I suffered the lash and walked in chains
Until the day I died.

My ailing mother never knew
The place of my demise,
No one grieved beside the grave
Or cared about her son.

A sentence for the term of life,
Perhaps it was deserved,
But even death brought no release
From this prison soil.

Cargo

(with acknowledgement to John Masefield)

Images of Nineveh from ancient Roman days,
A galley glides on silky seas towards a far shoreline,
Cargoes of exotica,
Creatures of rarity,
Perfumed woods and vessels full of sweet white wine.

Images of Nineveh from modern-day Iraq,
A car careers with vile intent towards the human flood,
Cargoes of bitterness,
Hatred, prejudice
Exploding on the streets full of rank red blood.

A Personal Affair

Achilles Heel

Do not go to Circe's isle
To watch her sorcery displays,
The sweet enchantment of her smile
May change you in capricious ways.
Do not stop at Lotus-land
To eat the luscious golden fruit,
Lest you forget the course you planned
And laze in dreamy disrepute.
Do not heed the Sirens' call,
Their silvery, seductive song,
Those that hear remain in thrall
And in that place their bones belong.
Oh, stop my ears and bind me to the mast
That I may keep my freedom to the last.

Dancing With Fire

The night I saw him dance a reel
With vigour, zest and style,
My senses thrilled from head to heel,
An image to beguile –
A first flutter of fancy.

Inviting me to dance a waltz,
He led me to the floor,
Aware of charms that could be false –
And yet I wanted more –
A first flurry of fluster.

And when I saw him rumba,
Entwined in syncopations,
His partner, who was younger,
Knew all the variations –
A first frisson of folly.

But then I joined him in a jive,
We made the dance floor shake,
Exhilarated nerves alive,
Sensations wide awake –
A first flicker of flame.

A smooth and sensuous cha cha,
We weaved and wound and flowed,
The heat and beat of that guitar
Burned cheeks until they glowed –
A first flush of fever.

The last dance was a tango,
We swooped and leaned and posed,
A vibrant, wild fandango
That warm desire exposed,
As final flames enclosed.

Just a Taste

Where's my equilibrium gone?
What's this odd forgetfulness?
These churning thoughts and longing sighs?
Absorbed in crazy daydreaming
I missed the turning on the drive to work.

A calm, contented life disturbed
By sweet excitement and intense desire.
I needed nothing: now I want it all.
So much upheaval in so little time
From just one evening in his company.

A Disturbing Drive

As I walked home from work,
A car drew up beside me,
I knew the company name,
I also knew who drove the car,
Though I had never met him,
Only heard he'd asked about me.

Soft tones reached me
Through the open window,
'Would you like a lift?'
Magnetised, I turned to see
The owner of this velvet voice
And felt my knees begin to melt.

His smile and unassuming air
Attracted me, yet he was no Adonis,
But like an eager heroine,
Breathless and with pounding heart,
I was irresistibly drawn
To this mild-mannered man.

Chemistry was in control;
Forgetting all advice
About cars and strange men,
Mesmerised, I slid
Into the passenger seat
And sensed his closeness.

This was a journey
That powered a passion.

Betrayed

Everything changed,
Once it was known.

Seductive secrecy,
Delicious danger,
Risk of revelation.

Deception brought spice,
Disclosure disenchantment,
Shorn of its power,
Now that it was known.

The Meeting

Love beckoned on a chill November day,
A swift and sudden call to be reborn,
The sight of you like blossom time in May,
The sound of you like birdsong at the dawn.
Nervous and shy, yet longing to be near,
Fearful of pain that love's desire can bring,
Unsure, unsteady, like a youthful deer,
I tiptoed through the bright, crisp world of spring.
Cautious of capture, alert to every sound,
I ventured down the winding path in view,
My timid steps were startled when I found
The way had led me face to face with you.
The doubts were stilled, for as we gazed awhile,
I saw the summer in your radiant smile.

Dream Lover

Just when I thought that it had passed
You slipped into my dreams
With your warm smile
And loving eyes
And tender touch.

Just when I thought I was immune
You reawakened passion's sighs
With your eager lips
And ardent gaze
And soft caress.

Just when I thought desire had died
You aroused erotic thrills
With your urgent kiss
And hungry look
And amorous hands.

Just when I felt a spreading warmth
You held me in intense embrace
And our panting mouths
And fevered glance
And clasping arms
And pounding hearts
And clinging thighs
And straining hips
And arching backs
And gasping cries
Brought the sweetest pleasure
That still haunts my dreams.

Invitation To a Dance

I had an invitation to a dance
And took for company a longtime friend,
I never dreamt that it would bring romance.

That he was free to go was purely chance,
For there were other parties to attend,
I had an invitation to a dance.

With charm and gentle humour to entrance,
A perfect escort – no need to pretend,
I never dreamt that it would bring romance.

A glowing warmth shone from his every glance,
What did that firm, yet tender touch intend?
I had an invitation to a dance.

While waltzing cheek to cheek, as in a trance,
I wondered what this closeness would portend,
I never dreamt that it would bring romance.

I could have had no inkling in advance
What an enchanting evening I would spend.
I had an invitation to a dance,
I never dreamt that it would bring romance.

Honey For Tea

Together in the cosy room,
Talking softly, sipping tea,
Sitting near – but not too close,
But close enough to fluster me.

A comfortable and friendly chat,
Exchanging looks with shining eyes,
'Well, I must go,' he says, and yet
That wish to stay he can't disguise.

A goodbye peck upon the cheek,
Then eyes are filled with warm desire,
Again the firm and tender touch
Of lips that hint of hidden fire.

And then a long and lingering kiss
That overwhelmed my breathing,
Delicious and demanding lips
That ravished all my being.

The Ruby Affair

Friends for forty years
And still a warmth of feeling,
Despite the times of tears,
Such closeness is appealing.

And still a warmth of feeling
Pervading this affair,
Such closeness is appealing
For this particular pair.

Pervading this affair
An easy intimacy,
For this particular pair
The need is to be free.

An easy intimacy,
Respect and high regard,
The need is to be free,
A compromise that's hard.

Respect and high regard,
Despite the times of tears,
A compromise that's hard –
Friends for forty years.

To Her Bold Lover

'To his Coy Mistress', by Andrew Marvell (seventeeenth-century English poet) – The Lady's Reply.

I thank you, Sir, for your sweet verse,
An invocation to coerce
This virgin lady who awaits
A swain who true love demonstrates.
You say that I am worth the time
To woo, while I am in my prime,
My coy reluctance you disparage,
But, Sir, you did not mention marriage.

The reason I withhold my favour,
Deny these wild delights to savour
Is when you have what you desire,
Your love may rapidly expire.
I will have lost a great attraction
For momentary satisfaction,
And what if our luxurious sport
Produced an infant to support?

'Tis easy, Sir, to be a man
And take your pleasures where you can,
Yet when you want to choose a wife,
You seek a lady of chaste life.
So your persuasions I refuse,
Even if your love I lose,
Today your passion is sincere,
Tomorrow you may disappear.

Epitaph

I miss you every day, my friend,
It seems you never leave my mind,
Close companion to the end.

Others cannot comprehend
Esoteric ties that bind,
I miss you every day, my friend.

Never needing to pretend
How my feelings were inclined,
Close companion to the end.

Our understanding could transcend
Communication most refined,
I miss you every day, my friend.

Precious time that we would spend
In those last years when you were blind,
Close companion to the end.

The one on whom I could depend,
It comes as no surprise to find
I miss you every day, my friend,
Close companion to the end.

The Empty Shell

A diagnosis on the day he died,
A tumour, they said,
Deep-seated,
Inoperable.

A victim of the concentration camp
Of cancer, they said.
Skeletal,
Cadaverous.

A sad, pathetic figure, old and frail,
So courteous, they said,
Dignified,
A gentleman.

A phone call chilling in its urgency,
Dying, they said.
Nature's cure,
No lingering.

A body he had once inhabited,
No suffering, they said.
A good death,
An empty shell.

Go In Peace

We did not always get along
And days before you died,
You made me rather angry –
My impulse was to chide.

But something told me, 'Leave it.
Don't spoil a pleasant day.
It's really not important
For you to have your say.'

When I saw you prostrate
And knew your fate was sealed.
My thoughts were kind and tender,
My irritation healed.

You went without a murmur,
A gentle, peaceful end,
Leaving me with no one
On whom I could depend.

A mother is a person
Whose love you can't erase.
That simple, deep devotion
I never can replace.

Intruder

I come with stealth,
Leave no trace,
Enter in silence,
Hide within.

A parasite
Laid in the living,
As I grow
I consume my host.

Believing you cannot be
One of the chosen,
You think
I will pass over you.
But I am there,
Dividing, spreading,
Unobtrusively,
        taking over
                your tissues.

Metamorphosis

She stood there on the doorstep,
With bright smile and jaunty air,
Lustrous curls cascading to her shoulders.

Was this
The girl I knew?

Her new sophistication startled me.
A poised, alluring twelve-year-old,
Who had a fresh awareness of herself.

Was this
The child I knew?

Then I saw her knowing eyes,
The youthful innocence was gone.
Changed forever by biology.

The girl I knew,
A child no more.

The Kindness of Memory

When there is good and bad,
We tend to remember the good,
People's idiosyncrasies –
Make us laugh –
Drive us mad.

We meet old friends
After many years,
Recalling only the laughter.

Confronted by tiresome habits –
Surprised we forgot them –
We practise patience.

We know we will soon forget
Vexations at friends' foibles,
The kindness of memory
Celebrates their spirit,
Values their virtues.

To Maddie

If there is any form of afterlife,
There is just one that I would want to meet,
Others could cause me grief or strife.

You, who made my life complete,
Would wait for me in rain or snow
Beside the gate, on cold concrete.

Although it was many years ago
You passed to that mysterious plane,
Your memory lingers here below.

I'd want forever to remain
If I could spend eternity with you
Enjoy your perfect company again.

So when I reach the gate I must pass through,
Be there, Maddie, for our rendezvous.

Out and About

The Bondi Minotaurs

(Display at the Sculpture by the Sea exhibition at Bondi, November 2006)

Modern Minotaurs
Lounge at the waterfall,
Sunbaking on rocks,
Posing provocatively,
Leaning nonchalantly
Against the boulders,
Bull heads peering,
Watching each other.

The scene is magnetic
To all that pass.

These mythic beings,
Almost human,
Bring from ancient Greece
A wry parody,
The star –
Narcissus.

Little Wattlebird

With a rattle and a squawk and a kak kak kak,
This bird was a lively fellow,
It bounced in the branches of a banksia tree,
As it supped on the blooms of yellow.

A boisterous, noisy, cheerful bird,
It looked like a madcap thrush,
All its grey feathers were speckled with white
To blend with the bottlebrush.

The harsh, discordant cadences
Would seem a handicap,
But the answering calls from a nearby shrub
Soon enticed this garrulous chap.

An attitude to emulate
From a bird so positive,
Despite its voice and dowdy look,
It knows the way to live.

Snack Lunch

She sat beside me in the bus shelter,
Enjoying the autumn sunshine,
Eating lunch from a paper bag.

Soft hair was tinged with red,
Brown eyes brimmed with vitality,
As deftly, daintily, she nibbled titbits.

A scruffy youth came slouching by,
Lost in sullen, resentful thought,
Muttering coarse oaths beneath his breath.

She stopped him in his shuffling tracks.
He stared – bewitched by her beauty,
And then a beaming smile transformed his face.

We watched her pick out tasty morsels,
Consume them with delicacy,
The metal shelter an enchanted wood.

She looked at us, her gaze questioning,
Squirrelling scraps into plump cheeks,
Then, at the sound of the bus,
She rippled up a nearby tree.

Flamingo Lake

In pink and white plumage
They flowed across the lake
In a corps de ballet
Choreographed by spring.

Like ballerinas on *pointes*
Their toes skimmed the water.
Heads, held high, bobbed
And turned from side to side,
As dancers chose their partners
For the season's *pas de deux*.

The Call of the Sea

Born and bred on an island,
Is that why I love the sea?
The soothing sound of breaking waves
Brings tranquillity.

I can sit on the beach for hours
Watching the ebb and flow,
Marvelling at the sense of peace
The rhythm can bestow.

Perhaps because of the water
I love the colour blue,
Clothes, home and possessions
Favour cerulean hue.

My star sign is earth, not water,
Yet I am drawn to the sea,
That salty scent and tang on the tongue
Stirs creativity.

From the cliffs or coastal pathway,
I follow the crashing waves,
Gushing their foam over the rocks,
Swirling into the caves.

Whenever I seek revival,
The ocean calls to me,
It renews and uplifts my spirit,
Restoring serenity.

Dressed To Thrill

The moon opened her wardrobe –
Gowns of silver, ivory, primrose –
She sighed at the delicate pastels,
Longed to look striking,
How she envied the rainbow.

Then she noticed the calendar –
Soon the earth's shadow would pass over her
When she was in her fullness.
'Ah!' she said, her spirit lifting,
'For the eclipse I shall wear burnt orange.'

The Magpie Choir

A little group of magpies,
All sleek in black and white,
Were waiting for their audience
To gather at the site.

When he saw the people
Watching curiously,
The leader gave a signal
And walked around the tree.

And all the magpies followed,
To gather in a troupe,
They looked towards the leader
To supervise their group.

Then the leader raised his head
And opened wide his beak,
From his throat came music that
To magpies is unique.

And all the birds joined in the song,
An eager warbling choir,
They filled the air with melody
For listeners to admire.

The audience stayed still and quiet,
Though wanting to applaud,
While little bits of biscuit
Were offered as reward.

The birds retreated to the bush
To eat their tasty snack.
Then took their audience by surprise,
Following their leader back.

Ready for an encore,
They came on stage again,
Performed their haunting cadences
Of silvery refrain.

This charming magpie chorus,
A musical cascade,
Transformed our simple picnic
With exquisite serenade.

Across the River

From my secret forest hideaway
I saw the tossing heads,
My heart was beating wildly in dismay,
The mares came down the mountain,
I was sure that one would fall
On that slippery and treacherous terrain.
But they reached the water safely
And I saw them hesitate,
Still propelled by their desire to be free,
Then they plunged into the river,
Felt the moisture on their flanks
And down my spine I sensed a sudden shiver.
With their nostrils raised and flaring,
Tresses flying in the spray,
They had the will and bearing
To escape the rider's chase,
And I hoped with all my being
That the mares would win the race.

Ode To Bright Eyes

Every year my English yard
Displayed scaevola flowers
In hanging baskets on the fence,
You bloomed, despite the showers.

I loved your mauve exuberance,
You almost seemed to dance,
Extending graceful sprays of stems
Adorned with petal fans.

You never needed pruning,
Never caused me stress,
Just drinking water every day
Maintained your loveliness.

And now I have you, Bright Eyes,
So high in my regard,
Spreading dainty flowers from pots
In my Australian yard.

Lighter Notes

The Reluctant Valentine

I wanted so much to send you a card
To tell of my love on Valentine's Day,
But I always find it so terribly hard
My intimate feelings to put on display.

So here is a verse to show my regard,
Perhaps in a poem I can portray
A show of affection you cannot discard,
But not too effusive to cause you dismay.

Yet now I feel my efforts ill-starred,
Passionate senses in disarray,
This undemonstrative lovelorn bard
Cannot put pen to paper today.

Georgy's Duties

To guard the home and territory
And keep the mistress company,
These duties are for any dog
Listed in the catalogue.

I think my most important task –
For which my mistress did not ask –
Is to ensure she wakes from sleep,
Especially when her slumber's deep.

So when the morning light appears,
I raise my head and cock my ears
To listen for that strange machine
That buzzes when it's eight-fifteen.

Then I'm up and full of zest
And even when she does protest,
I tap my paws upon her bed
Until she lifts her sleepy head.

I whimper, beg and prance about,
So she can have no further doubt
It's time to rise and start the day,
Get out of bed without delay.

Although she sighs and groans a bit,
She understands the benefit
And puts the biscuits in my bowl –
Wondering who is in control.

I know that there will be some talk
Before she's ready for my walk,
So while she listens to the news,
I'm back in bed to have a snooze.

Limericks

There was a young literary gent
Whose income gave cause for lament,
For a rude magazine
He wrote stories obscene,
But the silver did not bring content.

A poet in search of the muse
Decided to go on a cruise,
But each far away place
Brought only disgrace
Because he got hooked on the booze.

A novelist prim and demure
Wrote romances moral and pure,
But readers want sex
And writers need cheques,
So she put in some lust as a lure.

Highway Cheer

I am the highway snowman,
Beside the roadworks zone.
Reflectors are my buttons,
My hat's a traffic cone.

I smile at all the drivers
Who pass me on their way.
My cheerful, chubby figure
Helps brighten up their day.

Ode To Usury

(with acknowledgement to 'Ode To Autumn' by John Keats)

Season of gloom and falling finances,
        Close companion of the failing banks,
Conspiring with them how to bridge expanses
        Between our hopes and statements filled with
blanks.
To re-negotiate the mortgage loan,
        And cash those blue-chip stocks and shares
                To swell the funds, and plump the bank
account,
        And try to keep some money for our heirs.
Those low investment yields that make us groan,
Exotic holidays we must postpone,
        To keep liquidity is paramount.

Mammoth Creation

(Seen at the Sculpture by the Sea Exhibition at Bondi, November 2004)

A toilet bowl to make a mouth
And plastic rings a trunk,
Car mats were this giant's ears,
Its body made of junk.

The shape was most impressive,
It was quite life-size,
The curling trunk and splaying feet
Were rubbish in disguise.

A mass of screens and printers,
Electric goods galore,
The cables wound to make its tail,
A standing garbage store.

An ironing board and golf bag,
Keyboards, baskets, shoes,
Tusks composed of plastic,
An elephantine ruse.

On feet of dumped computers,
It stood so proud and firm,
Displaying fans and radios,
A scrapyard pachyderm.

Life Is Too Short To Clean the Ridges

Tiles with ridges make me weep,
They catch the dirt with every sweep,
Then down I go on hands and knees
To scrub and scour the trapped debris.

My kitchen floor has been transformed,
The cleaning ritual reformed,
For now I brush and mop with smiles
My brand new smooth and ridgeless tiles.

Creative Juice

A grape, freshly picked,
Pops into my head.
There it ripens
Till crushed
In the press of composition.

Left to ferment,
Strained and blended,
Matured in the mind,
It may be sweet or dry,
Palatable plonk,
Or just occasionally,
Verse of finest vintage.

www.ingramcontent.com/pod-product-compliance
Lightning Source LLC
Chambersburg PA
CBHW062159100526
44589CB00014B/1875